Also by Chris Hoffman:

The Hoop and the Tree (ecopsychology/self-help/spiritual)
On the Way (poetry)
Realization Point (poetry)
Cairns (poetry)

Son of the Earth

poems
by Chris Hoffman

SON OF THE EARTH
POEMS BY CHRIS HOFFMAN

iUniverse books may be ordered through booksellers or by contacting:

iUniverse
1663 Liberty Drive
Bloomington, IN 47403
www.iuniverse.com
844-349-9409

ISBN: 978-1-6632-3994-5 (sc)
ISBN: 978-1-6632-3995-2 (e)

Library of Congress Control Number: 2022909201

Print information available on the last page.

iUniverse rev. date: 05/18/2022

May this work be of benefit to all beings

All these ages, back to the misty dawn,
the poets and sages have been saying but one thing.
Our job is to find its truth in our own words.

The function of poetry
is to midwife the soul.

Contents

Emptying the Kitchen Compost Bucket on New Year's Day

Blue translucent sky today and sun,
no wind but abundant cold.
As my boots go munching across yesterday's snowfall,
my torso tilts slightly to the left,
counterbalancing the heavy, lidded, five-gallon
plastic bucket in my right hand.

A cornucopia of slops
plops into the big bin beside the garden—
rotting plate scrapings, banana peels, wadded tea bags—
reminders of weeks of fine food and companionship,
whose odor now is an earthy, almost-pleasant putrid,
far distant on the fragrance spectrum
from that of baking bread.
Our leavings now are ready for worms and microbes to enjoy
while making soil in which to grow fresh meals.

I add a comfortable layer of dry grass and dead leaves on top.
The tines of the pitchfork hum softly
through the shaft to my gloved hand.
I rinse the bucket in a clear stream of pre-icicle.
May the coming year be this full
of the sensuality of ordinary things.

Waterfall, Sounding

in this mountain stream, a pounding
fluent light—sleek, wet, curving—
pours ever new, never ending,
an insistent lustrous rush over
the dark rock drop.

It reveals itself as life does—
this and this, and then this and this—
emerging from primal fecundity
into tumult, into grace.

Its coursing braids together
reverence, dread, wonder.
How can I help but
bow in all directions?

Earth Sutra

Three mule deer browsing on a hillside
pause and turn their heads
to look at us with large brown eyes.

What do they see?

Can their gaze so bend
our own sight inward
that we see into the treasury
of our own experiences?

Holding a sleeping baby
close to your heart,
your arm under its bottom,
your hand on its back—
it gives itself to you completely.

Pure sleep.

Nothing sinks into you more deeply
than its manifest belief
that you are safety embodied
and utterly good—
the warmth and full weight of that experience,
and the lightness it brings.

And when that baby first entered the world
from between the gates of flesh
and the light first shone from its brow,
it was as though
a film of haze had been wiped away
from everything,
and everything shone.

At the seashore, flocks of little sandpipers
skitter along the lips of the speaking sea,
stamping foot tracks into the damp sand—
a vanishing cuneiform
of messages that all can see
but only a few will read.

And, far-ranging in the open oceans,
how do the people of the whale nations
view us? And how the stolid boulder?
And how the plashy stream
so musically descending?
For the earth is suffused, shot through
with aliveness, as shot silk
with iridescent threads.
And these three deer that look at us
are but three of many sensibilities
of the living earth on every continent
and in the sea and sky that see us.

In wiser times an initiated person
would wed the earth.
And in our weddings yet today
the veil is thin between our hearts
and the hearts of others—
each of us a molded lump
of the dough of creation,
where deep within the core of each
we can almost discern
the god-and-goddess dancing in a flame,
one of the shards of the primal fire.

And when the inn of the body
becomes vacant, before the body
sinks again into its elements
between the gates of earth
or through the appetite of fire,
at that transition moment
a door opens to a deep presence
which any gathered witness can feel.

When we fall out of delusion
we are caught by the safety net
held up by all our relatives—
the trees, the mosses, sunshine, rain,
rift valley, sea ice, fungi, chloroplasts,
gulch, krummholz, fertile field, gorilla, nighthawk:
this earth. We eat of it, breathe of it, drink of it,
are it.

To it we owe ourselves
by whatever name—José, Maria—
our languages, arts, and civilizations,
our bread for the body,
our bread for the soul.

It is said that externally
if you are attached to form,
internally your mind will be confused.
It seems our job
is to see with and through the earth
to what is good and beautiful
and true, and live that
and be unconfused.

The joy and sorrow of life
is that, like music with its flow of tones
and rhythmic punctuation,
the melody is ungraspable,
unavailable, unless time passes—time
that, like the rain,
falls on both the unjust and the just.
What we love passes away
or becomes something else
in the process of arriving.
The perfect cherry blossom wilts
and then the cherry swells
in time to be digested.

This very life burns to ash
like a stick of incense.
How is it possible to describe
the thunder gap
when everything suddenly
becomes the same as before
yet very different?

Throughout all our days
may we quench our thirst
at the spring of wonder.

Following the way,
in awe of its power,
may we find our true nature,
for there is no other place of refuge.

One hundred times fall down;
one hundred and one,
get up again.

May we awaken with all beings.

Chakra Incantation

For the sake of all beings
I wear the seer's tunic and hose
and raise my runic staff at night
toward where the moon in beauty glows.

I conjure the male and female energy snakes
to awaken at the root of my spine
and, entwining, to rise to the crown of my head
to form the androgynous vine.

The seven places the twins touch
blossom like magnificent flowers
into seven radiant cart's wheels of jewels
that are doorways to insight and power.

But the toll for crossing each threshold
is to leave some old chaff behind
and abandon some dear self-deceptions
that have cluttered the sight of the heart and the mind.

For the ascent is also a descent.
Each doorway is obscured by a veil
of greed, anger, and/or delusion.
The work is removing each veil.

Where the psyche weaves its mycelial threads
among the grains of mother matter,
deep in the realm of myth and metaphor
we perform our seven labors.

Decipher, O Goddess, the occult hieroglyphics
showing the way to the other shore,
tattooed above the curly foliage
arching over your most secret door.

Safely guide us through the seven gates:
open us to rootedness in good,
to skillful ways in sex and power and love,
in understanding and being understood,

and seeing with the eye behind the brow
that opens when the outer eyes are closed
like opening a door from within a darkened room
to see the garden of the perfect rose.

Let male and female serpents rise
to where the thousand-petaled lotus blooms
and—beyond this doorway—to the mystic union
of the holy sun and holy moon.

Sitting by the Lakeside Cottage

I look up from my book
past the gray weathered wood of the dock
to watch the playful breeze
scallop and reticulate the water
into a thousand and one wobbling dimples of light.

Up in the trees, the breeze
provokes a subtle shushing susurrus
among all the leaves outstretched
to accept the generous alms of sunlight.

The water of the lake laps and slurps
at the rounded rocks trimming the shore.
With the sun now fully out from behind a cloud,
myriad bright ripples school cheerily downwind.

From far across the lake,
punctuating the calm, come
seven smart hammer strikes
driving a nail home.

Then remain only the timeless
breeze on the lake,
the lapping water,
the trees.

Beginning Meditation

The match strikes,
fusses into blossom,
kisses the candle's wick
to a fluid wavering flame,
which ignites a stick of incense
to send sweet resinous fragrance
into the invisible.

We bow, sit quietly,
and extend the empty alms bowl
of the open soul.

We are offered
a complete serving
of this day
with its allures and tangles.

Many different scenes,
both beautiful and horrible,
appear at the mind's window.

At times we may hear
one or another of the three musics
granting tears, or joy, or rest.

Slowly we clear a space
in the quiet of the heart
where wisdom and love
can come and sit with us
and place a steady hand
on the helm of our being.

A Flight of Wings

Why do we gladden at a flight of wings,
or take long walks along an empty shore,
or visit with the sick or sick at heart?
For the sake of something vital at our core.

The soul's gold is not the common gold.
It is a treasure of a different kind—
a song remembered from the days of old,
companionable silence with a friend.

It is the pearl for which we gladly dive,
over and over, to keep it in our sight
because, without it, we would be as wanting
as day without its true companion: night.

Hand-fashioned, stitch by stitch, from acts of kindness
and suffering consciously endured—
from here we send our deepest prayers to mystery
and touch the earth to know when we are heard.

When unruly wind tousles fields of grass,
a third thing, neither grassy fields nor wind,
beyond the grasp of words but like a hidden
music, stirs and wakes us from within.

Since power and wealth and fame are not the goal,
what is the risk in living for the soul?

Walking into the Foothills in Autumn

So many seasons and years
have I walked this borderland.

Again I trace the thin trickle of a creek
from the fringe of the high prairie
toward a narrow cleft
at the base of the mountains.

The grassland gradually swells to rounded mounds
like a buffalo robe warming the toes of the foothills.
There is still a hint of green,
but the tall stems are all whisky-colored or Chablis.

Along the creek, the cottonwoods' foliage
is far gone from the verdant murmur of May
through the soft rustle of summer
toward the shaken brown rattle of late October.
By filtering sunlight, their leaves glow
in greens and yellows like stained glass.

Within a few hundred comfortable strides
the hills tower above me, thick with trees now—
ponderosa and some juniper—punctuated by crags
and slabs of conglomerate rock, pointing, almost vertical,
like the sterns of sinking ships,
some as big as sports fields: reddish rock
with scabs of lichen the color of weathered copper.

Today is such a day
as would make reincarnation
an appealing prospect.

In this season, all of us living beings
are preparing for the same winter.

You can smell the winter coming
and see it in the dark cadmium reds
of the sumac leaves
with their marshaled lance points,
and in the alluring vermilion of the poison ivy,
and in the pods of milkweed
curing to their necessary brittleness.

The same winter comes for all of us,
with all our different ways of being—
the cicada people, the magpie people,
the human people, the bear people—
all preparing for a changed world.

And I, preparing,
walk again into these foothills,
these ancient, ancient cloisters.

Since I will leave this world without pockets,
and as my body is curing to its own brittleness,
I wonder: What inner patterns have I ripened
that could pass with me beyond the veil?
And who will speak these words when I am gone?

So many years have I walked this borderland.
It is always the same; and yet it never is.

Ode to My Work Gloves

(Agradezco a Pablo Neruda)

My floppy grimy hand clothes
of split leather
and cotton canvas
full of all the dirt
I never
needed to wash away,
shiny and polished
in places
by long working
of the rake handle,
the hammer,
by cushioning for me
the sharp bite
of heavy boxes
and big pieces
of lumber—
selflessly,
over and over again,
you have warded off
splinters, calluses,
moon-like blisters,
while shaping yourselves
to the idiosyncrasies
of my left
and right
hands.

You call to mind
handprints
surviving
from archaic

ancestors
who pressed their hands,
wet with mineral paint,
on to the walls of caves
or under overhanging
cliffs
and, along with
those dexterous hands,
call to mind
all our history
of inventing,
using,
and naming
tools—
sharp rock,
stick of sound wood,
spade,
peavey, fid, and dibble,
noun and verb and syntax,
paper money,
trustworthy agreements,
knitting needles,
potter's wheel,
soldering iron,
stethoscope,
up through and including
digital computer—
that began
as counting on fingers—
and internet,
named after the fisherman's net
that is hauled in
with work gloves.

Along with all the old work,
there is new work
that arises
for each generation,
and new tools
will be needed.
May any new tool
be
as serviceable
and life-affirming
as these
humble
well-worn
work gloves.

On Pilgrimage

Coming to the old woman
sitting by the side of the road,
we crossed
from one side to the other
of the imaginary line
inside her head.

We bowed
and paid her one coin each.

She stamped our pilgrim passports.

Now she smiles and waves
as we walk on.

We are still smiling
and waving back.

Advice from the Last Loon

If you have ever heard my cry,
even once,
you still have not forgotten

that wild sweet yearning
for some indescribable paradise
shaken loose inside you.

I know what it is like to ride on a pillow
of blue water twinkling with sunstars,
with my youngster on my back
and my partner beside me.

I know the immutable dark green of the pines
and have seen stark winter branches
unfurl each spring their buds of green flame
into an amazement of foliage,
mad to sort the winds of any summer storm.

I know that joy takes many forms.

I know cold rain
and moody mornings
when the air hangs thick with mists.

I know the long dive in clear clean water
and the skill of the catch
and the satisfaction of feeding one's constant companion,
hunger.

And in my many lives
I have known the closing of the eye
and have felt the teeth of fox
pierce my body.

I know the utter stillness of deep nights
far removed from human commotion.

And I have seen when colder days
splash burning reds and startling yellows
over my neighbors, the hills.

All of this, my life,
I put into my cry.

And, as I am the last of my kind,
I make this request:

Carry my cry with you
as you travel through desperate times
into the future,
as in your many stories of an ark
carrying life safely through a flood.

What my cry has touched in you
is the source of your gift.

Live my cry
when you work to heal the world.

The American Pika

who is a cautious small bundle of fur,
knows how to survive the bitter winter
in its high mountain mansion
of granite rockfall crevices
by gathering hay
all the brief summer.

Can you do that?

The Creator, they say,
distributed the wisdom all around
so humans would not become
too arrogant
by knowing everything.

But our current arrogance
is heating the planet so much
that we are forcing the pika
higher and higher on the mountain
towards the summit,
where the mountain will end
and, with it, the pika.

I say we must be
humble and respectful
in the presence of every member
of creation, because
we don't know who might appear
when we die
to guide us
on the next part of our journey.

Kintsugi
("kin-tsu-gi")

Another day of political action
and the good feeling of working
with friends old and new
to make the world a better place.

Another day of political action,
exiled from the hearts
of other human beings
who seem unbothered by hatred
or the impending end of the habitable world,
but who are suffering in other ways.

I search for an image
of how we could be
if we make it through these times.

I think it could be *kintsugi*—
the Japanese art of precious scars:
repairing broken pottery
while making it strong again and sagely beautiful
by bringing the broken pieces back together
with golden joinery.

The Net

Our hands are on the rim of a circular net.
You and I, together with others
who stand all around the rim of the net,
hold the net to form our circle.

We, and those who came before us,
have woven the net with strings
in a rainbow of colors. We are still weaving,
forming each knot with care.

The spirits of those who came before
stand behind us—watching, hoping, encouraging.
The spirits of those who will come after
are also watching, hoping, encouraging.

May our hands be strong to hold on.
May our fingers be dexterous with the flowing strings.
May we know that wherever others touch the rim,
each is doing their best with what they have been given.

We weave to renew the net for dear life
because, at its center, the net
holds and protects our planet
and all that we love about it.

We Have This Day

When I look at the world
these days, sometimes
I actually see it.

Where there are clouds adrift
in the lustrous evening sky,
I see clouds.

My plate of food
with its fragrances and colors
appears
as though I had never
seen it before.
Each bite is something new.

As we age,
my wife is more beautiful than ever
because of who she is.

In this life
we find ourselves
somewhere
along the axis
between the unspeakable
and the unnameable,
cupping our hands
around a precious flame.

The Old Language

If we could sit together sometime on a hillside
with vistas at our feet, a giant boulder at our backs,
comfortable to relax against
when we pad it with our packs,

And if we could converse together slowly
over a lengthening afternoon
while sharing wine or water, bread,
until we noticed the moon,

And if we could practice that old art
of speaking simply what seems true
for each of us as it springs from the heart,
still fresh with the energy of its making,
then we might hear each other's sorrows
as though it were our own heart breaking.

Then the me of me and the you of you
would soon discover, like brothers
returning from opposite and distant lands,
how best to join hands.

Spiritual Landscape

It can happen at the seashore
where the broad expanse of ocean
takes our vision on a far journey
into the vanishing distance
while we remain standing by the tide pool
with its sharp barnacles, slippery seaweed,
strange sea stars, and tiny scrabbling crabs.

It can happen at a spring-fed lake
surrounded by miles and miles of rolling grassland
where this year's new green is coming on,
smelling sweet, and where the loudest sounds
are the faint thrumming of insects,
the flutter of birds' wings, the occasional song,
and the plop of a frog in the water.

It can happen after walking
a long time in the high desert,
following a path that winds over and among
galleries of sensuously sculpted slickrock,
then sitting down in the shade of a pinion pine
for a drink of water, where what happens
is like finding in the sand nearby
a small drop of turquoise
as powerful as the whole sky.

It can happen at a tarn in the mountains,
or at a lake in the forest
where mink and kingfisher
come to drink, or when
our hand caresses
the textured bark and solid trunk of a tree
already many ages older
than our own hoped-for oldest lifetime.

It can happen wherever the air
is clean and pure
and wherever our innate sense
of rightness and beauty
awakens and pays attention.

Then we become an ear of listening,
and the whole world around us, too,
becomes an ear of listening.

The secret door opens
and we can go and come
with equal ease.

There's a Place

There's a place by the river
where the trees whisper gently.
It will take your sorrows away.

There's a song that resides
in the depths of the fiddle.
It will take your sorrows away.

There's a promise of love
that will never be broken.
It will take your sorrows away.

Through illness or death
or far separation,
as surely as night foretells day,

when your heart finds your place
in the mystery of being,
it will take your sorrows away.

I Take My Pulse

to diagnose my condition.
"Old age," I mutter—
"a serious case of it.
Probably terminal.
Who would have thought
it would come on this soon?"

In the One-room Hut

of our innermost life,
we live as a monk or a nun,
or as a monastic
of another variation of gender,
at the center
of the encircling universe.

We keep a candle burning
on the altar
of our big question.
We listen carefully.

At some precise moment
we blow out the candle
and step into the clear night
to breathe the blessed air
and experience the being of all being
in the company of the boundless field of stars.

What Could Be Better

than having your best beloved beside you
through the hours of hardship and delight
while holding on to each other's hand
in that certain way
that says we'd do it all over again.

Touching

In the chopping of vegetables—
potatoes, say, in their jackets coarse or smooth;
in the handling of chili peppers,
so scarlet and so lewd;
or in touching the skins of vivid green limes;
in the folding of laundry clean from the clothesline,
scented with sunshine and fresh air;
in the pulling of weeds from the garden;
in the washing of my own hands
or the hands of my young child,
I am also touching,
one after another, the prayer beads
of the feminine side of the holy.

In our round of days, in our round of years,
we finger a charm bracelet
of keepsakes and little silver skulls—
beads of sorrow and amazement—
through the telling of which
we enter into the mystery of the great round
and learn to offer our lives
as a garland of flowers
from our garden of earthly delights
to the one who has mothered us
all the way back
since the first unstruck sound.

Both mother-of-pearl
and pearl of great price,
she is the tenderness inside of grief
and the urge to nourish and protect
inside of adoration.

Wherever we go—
be it walking on the land,
sailing the seas, or flying through the air—
we are already in her temple.
The holy sites scattered here and there
are just to remind us
to remove our shoes from time to time,
bow our heads, and pay attention.

When we do so,
she unfolds to us the folds
of her many-folded, all-bestowing cloak,
revealing a cluster of roses
even in the midst of winter,
even in drought,
even in grief and fear and despair,
we are enfolded.

As we touch the world,
so are we touched.

The Pandemic

is alchemic.
It's a spiritual centrifuge

spinning at ten thousand RPM
in the laboratory of life,

rapidly clarifying the distinction
between the essence and the dross,

helping us awaken
from the nightmare of feeling separate.
We see more clearly

that what we're doing to the earth now
is spousal abuse,
and it hurts all our children;

other people
with their gifts and flaws
are just our other selves.

If we practice our lives
with attention,
we can transform:

From root to crown, inhale integrity;
exhale right relationship
in ever-widening circles.

Wisdom and compassion—the true gold.

The Spirit Blanket

What is the pattern
on the spirit blanket
that all these years
you have been weaving
on your inner loom?

There, in the sanctuary of the heart,
where the sweetest, most poignant music
can blossom from a mere whisper
of your secret wish,
there you are at work,
contemplating the mystery
of the pattern that wants to emerge.

Bless all who taught you
how to assemble
the pieces of your loom,
and those who showed you
where to place your fingers
as on a guitar or violin.

Every inhalation and exhalation
spins the thread for your work.

The juices of berries,
tinctures of earth and sky—
all you have ever seen and wondered at
in the natural world
has given you the wherewithal
to dye your thread
with many colors.

Now there is a rainbow overhead
showing the span of your life.
Perhaps the rainbow is also in your blanket,
where it arches over the woven symbol
for that which always
leads to your true home.

Surrounding that primary place
are the holy spirit beings
of north, south, east, and west,
who have come to be with you
in your dreams and ceremonies,
woven along with the dark threads
of heartache, grief, and sorrow.

Seeing this,
your mind sits down quietly
to be with your medicine—the gift
your life has been created to deliver.
When you sit with your medicine,
rings of blessing ripple outward
to create good cause in this world.

When your body lies down
for the very last time,
what is drawn up over your body
and the rest of your world
will be your spirit blanket.

The Counselors of the Heart

The heart has four counselors
who whisper advice.

The earth counselor
speaks of being present in the world.
The counselor of fire
lifts a guiding torch.
The air counselor
is the seer, always ingenious.
The counselor of water
brings jars of emotions from the well.

And then, at nightfall,
when the heart and all its counselors
are talking things over
around the campfire,

some wild dreams ride in
on horseback, dismount,
and recount strange entrancing tales
from exotic lands.

Cicadas

Sometimes I hear you
in the busy cicadas simmering
near the end of summer.

And then you fall silent
with the cicadas still simmering,
and it is only the heat.

This long depth
out of which I have climbed
in order to be here

leads from that same nothing
that has given us also
the cicadas and the fertile fields of the earth.

Wherever I turn,
it seems I have just missed
catching a glimpse of your face,

but then you pour through me
as a sudden quiver of recognition,
and I praise the simmering of the cicadas.

Drifting to Sleep

late at night,
I rouse briefly to the faint sounds
of a train's horn calling in the distance.
The sounds evoke simultaneous yearnings—
for roads not yet traveled and
for the comforts of home.
I snuggle more deeply
under my patchwork quilt
of happy memories
and dream of painting the wind.

Wampum

When we enter our important dreams,
we row across dark water
to reach the old world of myth.

On our way, one night, we might spy
a storytelling belt of wampum beads
floating on the water.

Each bead is the experience
of one of our days,
and the whole pattern is our life story.

Carefully we fish it out of the water
and bring it with us
in its glistening beauty.

At the marketplace on the far shore,
is there anything for which we would trade
this life of ours?

Drinking Tea Together

from a matched pair
of five-hundred-year-old
glazed earthenware cups—

How many whispering lips
have touched these rims?
How many intimacies have been shared
above the rising steam?

For My Wife

The spirit that animates you
is like a wise eagle—
far-seeing,
fiercely protective
of her mate and her young.

I can never really know
where you journey within,
or see the territory you cover
in your wide-ranging dreams
or in the prayers of your heart.

But I see clearly every day
your goodness,
your inner and outer beauty.

I come to you
still putting the pieces
of myself together.
I come from dark earth, from mud
and ancient mythologies,
from urgent blood
and a quest for healing beauty.

And every day
I seem to
imagine myself anew.

You take me
into the safe harbor
of your love.
You see me deeply.

When your hand
touches my cheek,
for me
nothing else exists
or needs to exist.

We have made ways
to be with each other
that no one else
could ever understand.

Our lives
are intertwined now
like a braid of sweetgrass,
and we burn
with one smoke.

I would be
your true husband
forever.

Standing on the Deck of the Ferry

watching the pier move away and farther away
behind the white and green foam
of our wake
is like reading old love letters
or looking again at old photographs
and remembering so much
of the love we had then
while watching the gap of years widen.

If I could not take your hand now,
I don't know what I would do.

From Parents to Children

We have tried to prepare you for this.
We love you. We trust you.
May the syllables of *ah!* and *yes!*
live in your hearts.
Run with gratitude.
Here's the baton.

My Son in the World

The story once had me at its center,
and still does; but now it is less solid.
Tendrils of my life drift away
like the smoke from a stick of incense.

I see my son moving out into the world
like one of those tiny human figures
in classic Chinese landscape paintings—
with the protagonist and his companion
pausing to contemplate some craggy cliffs,
some weather-beaten trees,
suggested by a few deft brushstrokes,
dwarfed by immense hills and distant peaks
that seem to float among the clouds—
almost clouds themselves—
with the path turning into vanishing
as it winds beyond the cloud mountains
into the untouched rice paper
with its unforeseen events and sights.

It reminds me of a path I've traveled;
but it is different. And with good fortune
he will see beyond and farther
from the crests of hills that I will never reach.

I wish for him eureka moments
and years of knowing himself to be a mensch.

And I hope that one day
when he reaches into his psychospiritual toolkit,
beneath the star charts, compass, stories,
field notebook, crystals, poems, pliers,
amulets, measuring tape, binoculars,

assorted screws and prayers,
he will spy,
carved in a hidden place,
the initials of his father and
his grand- and great-grandfathers—
all the way back—and, smiling inwardly,
will carve his initials there too
and share it forward.

Hush Now

Summer night is coming on.

The steady pulsing of trilling crickets
forms a curtain of sound
through which we pass
into a deeper night.

There, the immense two-horned moon
scything brightly
toward the western horizon
ornaments the flowing hair
of the masculine
half of divinity,
while the feminine half
conjures up the water lily blossom
of the rising sun,
which floats above her upraised palm.

As this two-in-one
sees deeply
from within our heart of hearts
and smiles the knowing smile
shared by the long-married,
night passes into day.

Regardless of what may happen next,
everything is clear.

The Eye of the Universe

When you truly perceive beauty,
you find yourself
looking into the eye of the universe,

which, you discover,
is looking directly
back at you.

Its pupil widens,
seeing
that something has changed.

It has been watching you
your entire life,
perceiving the marrow of your being.

Everything is different now—
more real,
though still the same.

You glimpse the exquisite lacework
linking all things
at their core.

Seeing deeply
through this eye
unties the obstinate knot.

The one who wears your name
emerges, like everything else,
from the hub of the turning wheel.

Hay for Monet

Scattered on the shorn field,
big rolls of hay
blush at the first light of dawn.

Hour by hour the light-giver
paints the day.
Clouds materialize, vanish.

Scattered on the shorn field,
silent rolls of hay sit
as though in meditation.

Calm rolls of hay
unfurl, shade by shade,
their vast repertoire of hues.

Gleaming rolls of hay, midday—
under their immense weight,
shadows hide.

As the shadows creep out
and lengthen toward night,
the hayfield rests.

Under the stars—
a harvest constellation:
big rolls of hay.

Between Two Trees

Between any two trees
the gap or space
forms a doorway.

On this side you inhale and exhale.
And on the other side
you inhale and exhale.

But to step through between them
with your mind alert and still
skims away distractions,
opens your inner eye.

You pass from this
into the *presence* of this.
Everything is a doorway.

Interlude: Pebbles

Flowering yucca—
a cascade
of parchment bells.

❦

It is so quiet in the slot canyon
that you can hear the wishes
the wings make in the air
as the raven flies by.

❦

Your absence has run me through
like a needle through a piece of cloth,
stitching me closer to you.

❦

Imagine returning as a mountain flower
beside this long, elegant pour—
pure satin, then sparkling beads.

❦

How long
does being here
take?

❦

Backcountry skiing, January—
cold sandwich, thermos of hot soup,
the blaze of snow.

CB

Stars in the void—
the scattered fragments
of our original eggshell.

CB

All along the dry grass path,
tiny Zen clackers clacking—
grasshoppers announcing summer's end.

CB

He went for a long walk
to discover
his feet.

CB

The best water of all—
powder snow tasted carefully
from the needles of a fir.

CB

The dented
galvanized iron watering can
sprinkles wrinkled water.

CB

From men's nipples too—
the milk
of human kindness.

ෆ

You may not be the relay runner,
but rather the fire
passed from torch to torch.

ෆ

The resting dog lifts her head,
reads the news
with her nose.

ෆ

When first I saw my true love's face,
a star shone at her brow.
And I would grieve ten thousand years
if she should leave me now.

ෆ

What do you say
to the congregation of yourself
when you stand at the pulpit
and look into those hopeful faces?

ෆ

Squat persimmon radiating
the color orange,
snow outside the window.

ଓ

In my dream
I tell my own story over and over again
until I get it right.

ଓ

The sounds of good music
form a beaded curtain.
On the other side
your beloved awaits.

ଓ

Four names in a lifetime:
Little Raven Feather,
Gleaming Raven Feather,
Wise Raven Feather,
Raven at Night.

ଓ

Looking at the world
from the other side of my mind
for a change,
I am astonished to see
what the bossy side of my mind
had taken for reality.

ଔ

All along the rocky shore
the ocean lavishly lashes,
before we arrive, after we leave.

ଔ

Some pieces of music
are birth canals.

ଔ

Live with an open heart.
You are married to time
till death do you part.

Howdy, Pardner

Did I ever tell you about the time
I fought Cowboy Death?

It happened in the desert on a clear night,
cold enough that I was glad to own a bedroll.

There was a full moon
that dusted the mesa cliffs with silver and rose gold.

(Mind you, this happened in another time,
in the time beside time.)

In all that silence and raw beauty,
I sat for a while after dinner in meditation.

My cushion was just my rolled-up bedroll
resting on my worn but still colorful Mexican blanket.

From time to time I heard a snap
and watched sparks from my campfire shoot up to the stars.

Despite the moon, the stars that night
were as many as a fistful of salt

spilled out on my black cast-iron skillet.
After buttoning-up camp for the night,

I snuggled into my bedroll to watch the sky.
Looking up as the person I was that night

made me feel happy and good.
The sky reminded me of one of those medicine

sand paintings that the People make. All the connections that could
explain the world to me were almost visible.

Suddenly the sky zipped open
along a spider's web of glowing lines,

showing me a vision: the sky as a yarn painting
in electric colors, horizon to horizon—

too complex to memorize completely
but unforgettable.

Perhaps it was a diagram
for the assembly of the soul.

So there I was,
trying to make sense of all this, when—

imagine my shock to see in the distance,
galloping straight at me,

a horse with a bare-chested skeleton for a rider
in boots, jeans, a big silver belt buckle, bandanna, and ten-gallon hat.

His eyes were glowing like coals,
and I could see he was grinning at me.

Imagine my shock!
He had chosen such a cliché!

As was true of his business card, too—
Tarot number thirteen: the card of Death.

"Howdy, pardner," he said, as he dismounted
and handed me his card.

"I'm here to make a bet: I'll give you five sheep
and a personal favor of your choosing

if you can jump through Window Rock
in a single jump

and jump right back through again on the next jump."
(Remember, this was in another time,

when Window Rock did not yet have its city
and the Rock itself was a place of ceremony.)

"And if I can't?" I asked.
"I'll take your immortal soul," he said.

"That's a stiff wager," said I.
"You don't have much choice," said Cowboy Death.

Then the two of us, together with my whole campsite—
including unperturbed horse, bedroll, and flickering campfire:

the whole kit and caboodle—were set right down
conveniently close to Window Rock.

Moonlight caressed the ponderous sandstone;
and through the enormous round window I could see more stars.

"Well?" said Cowboy Death.
I looked at the powerful rock with its window

and calculated my chance of success
to be approximately zero.

I was starting to thank my immortal soul
for its years of faithful service

and was about to give it its gold watch
when I had a spectacular idea:

"So, Mister Cowboy Death," I began,
trying to sound innocent,

"if I jump really fast, how will you
be certain that I've actually done it?"

"Aha," said Cowboy Death. "There's a little twig
on the far side where you're supposed to land.

"If I see the twig gets broken,
you win."

Now all I had to do
was to ask a spirit helper

to go where my body couldn't—
the easy part—

and snap a twig there.
That part would be more difficult.

Knowing this, I began to wonder:
of all the world's many manifestations of divinity,

with whom was I in good enough graces
that I could ask for such a thing?

As I was running through the list in my mind,
suddenly, like a flash of heat lightning,

the two-in-one spirit
took pity on me,

appeared from within the Ute Mountains
in her-and-his radiant feathers and dance kilt,

moccasins, turquoise and silver jewelry,
and made the jump for me as a gift,

then vanished like echoing thunder.
Even today I am speechless with gratitude.

Twig snapped.
I was free.

I also won five sheep and a personal favor
of my choice from Cowboy Death.

Cowboy Death was angry.
He gnashed his teeth and they fell out,

so he put them back in again.
"I'll get you in the end," he said.

"I know that, sir," I said. "I am of the nature to die.
There is no way I can escape death."

"As the Buddha would have us remember:
I will be separated from everything and everyone.

"My deeds are my only companions.
They are the ground on which I stand.

"So, Mister Cowboy Death, as my personal favor,
when you come again in the end, please make my death a good one."

Deep Song

When notes stream out
from the pregnant sound hole of a guitar
like a murmuration of starlings—
swirling, pulsing, narrowing, billowing—
or when sweetness flows
from the aching dark hollow inside a flute
or from yearning panpipes
made of reeds uprooted and cut,
when women in dangerously red dresses
and black high heels stomp on their demons,
causing frilly hems to lift and cascade
again and again as liquid pure seduction,
when primal thumping on a drum
makes its heartbeat known,
I keenly feel my love and sorrow
for you and me
and all that lives and dies.
This music is like the friendly roughness
found by a match
that opens the way for its pent-up flame.

Sitting in the Cathedral
(Cuenca, Ecuador)

In this house of awed silence
only a doorway apart from the hubbub of the world,
what is it toward which we look? What is
under this gilded half dome intimating sunrise
that is supported by four towering columns,
muscular with carved ropy spirals
ascending, descending,
also gleaming with gold?

Certainly more than the devotional image
beneath this half dome, within these columns.
And more, even, than the implicit story
of love, sacrifice, and redemption.

We look for a moment of transparency—
to see beyond and through the apparatus of life
to the underlying fibers and patterns,
to the warp and the weft, and our place in it,
to see as though from walking a ridgeline
with the beautiful wide green earth
cleaving away on either side.

We look for the scales to fall away from our senses,
to hear anew the ordinary daily conversations,
to smell the odors of cooking, and in the market place
to see the heaps of fruit with their colors,
the bags of rice, the mounds of potatoes,

to know that we are loved
and to know what we should do.

Eternity rains down upon us
as droplets of time.

And the person kneeling in the next pew,
just like us,
also wants to be happy.

Breath

In just a single
inhalation and exhalation
of breath,
the world convenes.

Off the west coast of Scotland
seals have hauled themselves
from the cold, glass-clear waters
of the North Atlantic
to nap on rocky skerries.

On the great plains of North America
a horse shakes its head
and ripples its skin
to dislodge a fly.

At a market stall in Africa
a wrinkled banknote
and a few coins
are given from hand to hand.

If it is nighttime,
somewhere in Central America
there is a parade of lights
with marching bands
and floats, and the local police car
decorated with lights,
and the scent of grilled meat,
and the fluorescent pinks and blues
of cotton candy,
the applause of the crowds.

Elsewhere, commuters
are squeezing into subway cars,
pressing close together
while shrinking inwardly
away from their own skins.

Along a ridgeline
in the Rocky Mountains,
a powerful wind blows wisps of snow
that sparkle and vanish
from the knife edge of a cornice.

A solitary bee
burrows into the dirt.

And in a concert hall somewhere,
after a magnificent flight
with Grieg's piano concerto,
soloist and orchestra, working together,
bring it in for a landing.

So, with every breath
there is the telling
of the infinite beads
of the world's rosary,

all threaded
on the subtle wind
that ensouls us all.

My Invisible Self

keeps arranging certain experiences
for me in this world
so that if I pay attention,
I might discover the myth
that is trying to live itself out
through me.

Once I discover that,
then between the myth and me
there is room for negotiation.

Go Down

In the dell of winter,
the going-within time,
when all the verdant juices of life
have withdrawn to roots and tubers underground,
we may find ourselves going down
into the quick of things.

There, energetic treasure lies,
which to the human eye
might look like pirates' chests
spilling over with ropes of pearls;
heaps of sunny topaz and other precious gems;
strange and mystical objects
worked from gold and silver;
and hermetic manuscripts
glowing with insight and revelation.

There it can seem
that a clear crystal
at the tip of a staff carven with images
touches a packed globe of glistening seeds
resembling the arils of a pomegranate,
and it flashes fire.

A great teacher once said
that if you bring forth
that which you have within you,
what you bring forth
will save you.

So ring out your inner music
from what is dark and fruitfully empty,
like the clapper in a bell.
"Ding-dong, ding-dong," it sings.
"The bucket would be useless
were it not for the well."

What Appears to Be So

When I watch the sun go down
beneath its splendid parachute of colors,
I bow to the west
and cherish the seasons of my life.

Somewhere in a kiva underground
I am also sitting with the spirits of all beings—
plant and animal and human—
and together we look up at ourselves
playing our roles in the world above,
in our costumes of species and gender;
and we watch in wonder.

Once, just recently long ago,
I had thought
that the kernel of my being
was a problem nut to be cracked open.
But instead
it appears to be the process itself
of sprouting.

The fascinating dance of gender
appears to be twin columns of smoke
twining upward around each other
from a single central fire.

There appears to be a bottomless well
of the purest dark water;
and the work of the one
who carries my name
is to pull on the rope
and raise the bucket
for the quenching of thirst.

I am just an old bear
watching a sunset,
remembering all the directions
toward which I have bowed,
cradling in the fondness of my heart
my mate and our cub,
the coming generations,
and this dying and living world
so worthy of praise.

Two Moons

is the name of the Cheyenne chief
photographed in 1910 by Edward Curtis.

Two Moons watches me from an old wall calendar.
We have studied each other for more than thirty-six years.

When I sit at my writing place and look up,
I see him looking back knowingly.

Early on, he looked just like my grandfather,
whom I loved and who was a guide for me.

Later, Two Moons seemed old enough
to be my father. I loved him too.

Now that all these men have passed beyond,
Two Moons looks like me.

He seems to see me more directly
every day.

And now I listen
for what my heart might want to say

when I leave to join them
at their council fire.

I Surrender

I have just a skeletal understanding
of death.

I have sat with the dying
and been at my father's side
when he passed.

But as to what it is really like
from the inside,
I can only speculate.

Is it like a ball of white-hot iron
that you have to grasp with both hands?

Is there a column of soft blue light
containing tiny golden droplets,
spirally descending and ascending,
that are actually souls
arriving from and departing for
our truest home?

Is it simply
the final exhalation of breath,
the final yogic corpse pose?

Is it
what we have been rehearsing
our whole lives
after every sexual climax,
in every deep meditation?

And if anyone comes
to lift us away,
who might that be?

All I can do
is say to the secret
that has led me this far:
"I surrender."

Crossing Over

At the mountain pass at the far frontier,
the ancient wise one says to the only guard,
"Please hold my cloak,"
then steps out of it
into invisibility,
following the way of all things.

Embroidered on the lining of the cloak
in golden threads
are words that circle
very close to the Tao.

Snow begins to fall
through the stainless air.

A Single Molecule

Set aside for the moment
your opinion,
your condition,
your situation.
Put a bookmark in the place
you know so well
that you can always return here.

By setting these things down
completely,
you are free to step back
and take your royal ease
on the jeweled seat of knowing.

Observe the limpid expanse of space
across which the mated swans of time
are gliding gracefully.

The flower you hold with your fingertips
is the kaleidoscopic blossom of perfection.
Its fragrance confirms your deepest hunch.

Watch as the nature
of the great As-Is
settles around you
into one of its infinite patterns of beauty,
while the four counselors of the heart
pour the waters of life
into the vessel of your wonder.

What you are able to bring back from this
is only a fragment
of what you have experienced.

But, being composed
of the atoms
of vision, love, and courage,
even a single molecule of hope
is powerful medicine.

As a Gift

I offer to you an all-night retreat
in the refuge of flowers,
far from the busyness of the world,
where you will be completely safe,
where, by candlelight, you can lay out
all the pieces of the puzzle of yourself
and observe a wiser hand
arrange them in a surprising and fulfilling way
as you are carried through the night hours
by a caravan of perfect music.
You settle back into the clarity
before thinking, discovering the wider view.
Then the four who witness all
make the sign of truth over your soul.

Taking Flight

In this remote place
of expectant quiet,
under the endless stars,
the head shaman sets the bullroarer
whizz-buzzing overhead,
swinging it in wide circles.

Invisibly, this clears
an opening right here
to the passageway
of no time to all places.

Through this opening
in the ceremonial now,
mysteries
become briefly accessible
while the bullroarer rests.

Filled with excitement and dread,
we stand ready
in our shimmering feathered
costumes of transformation.

The most experienced ones of our group
take flight first.

We beginning students
stumble into becoming airborne
and follow, closely watching
how the best ones do it.

We hope to be like them
and come back safely,
wiser and more humble.

We fly to pass beyond our fears
and to receive teaching
from the great wisdom
that causes
truth and beauty and peace
to dawn in our hearts.

Later, we learn
that the bullroarer,
when it speaks again
with its zippering sound
and blurred circles,
is also the lure
that we listen and watch for
as we fly in our bird skins and feathers,
seeking the way home.

Snow

Snow on the ground,
brilliant and melting in sunshine—
the days are lengthening.

During the longest night of winter,
in the dark, at midnight,
when the boat seemed surely to be sinking,
the ineffable
appeared in a mask of stunning beauty
and spoke the first word of instruction
of how to move forward,
instruction that continues
as the sunshine
and the melting of snow.

Night by the Ocean

The ocean's waves
bow gracefully to the shore,
offering garlands of seaweed
and pieces of broken shell

in ongoing tribute
to the massive land,
whose mountains and rivers
channel all of their waters
to nurture the sea.

What beauty is equal
to spending an evening by the wild ocean
as its waves crush and hush,
then crush again
with endless lush ablutions,

while knowing that vast tonnage of water
to be invisibly fuller of life-forms
than a whole human lifetime
is full of fleeting thoughts and feelings,

and seeing the flawed pearl
of the round moon—
so out of reach—
place glittering flecks of light
across the dark and rumpling water
like a path of possible steppingstones
to gain the heart's desire.

The Cave of Unknowing

When at last you enter the cave of unknowing
and find your way to the other world
ever present beside our own,
you will step out on the other side
into the vivid night wearing nothing
but those terrifying and exhilarating ceremonial clothes
that reveal the beautiful intricacies of your soul.

Your guide will lead you through the wilderness.
Sometimes it will feel like going farther and farther down
into the deepest darkness on rickety ladders.

You will pass the grim mask
of the fear of death
on your way to a circle of people around a fire
waiting for you under the stars.

They sing you welcome,
using for you the same name
you use for yourself
when you are all alone,
contemplating
a palmful of earth.

In the faces that turn to you—
a cross section of humanity, of ages, races, and genders—
you will see nothing but love and acceptance.

Everyone you'd hoped would be here, is.
And all the rest, and all your spirit allies.
This is your circle; they see you thoroughly.

You will lie down on a bed of boughs
and soft blankets,
comfortably warm near the fire.

A priestess holding a black feather
and a priest holding a white feather
will work down your body, head to toe,
wafting harmful energies into the fire
where they burn away,
transformed into fragrant smoke.

You will close your eyes
and hear music so beautiful,
you will weep with joy.

Heartache,
heartache,
adios.
Heartache,
heartache,
adios.
Heartache, O heartache,
heartache, O heartache,
heartache,
O heartache,
adios.

It will be startling—
like looking into a mirror
and suddenly seeing through it,
as through a window,
your original face
before even your parents were born.

The feathers brushing over you
will sound like the wind that shakes the barley
and be as gentle as a small cloud in good weather.
Your inner landscape
will begin to smile in hues and colors
as it embraces dawn.
You may feel like a fine work of pottery
newly splashed with glaze
and freshly fired.

When you open your eyes, you will find
your hands placed together in prayer,
holding one black-and-white eagle feather
that represents your inner union,
all the parts of you, all the wisdoms joined,
together now and present here.

Along the return journey
you will pass
the mask of the death of fear.

It's a Funny Thing

The quieter you become,
the more clearly the path shines.
The noise of the mind
obscures the path.
The mind is useful to a point
like a rowboat with its oars.
You arrive at the middle of the lake.
When the ripples subside,
the image of the moon
floats on the water.

Blessingway

May you be carried comfortably,
as though drifting downstream
on a cushion of music.

And when you look up,
may you see revealed
in the dome of the sky
the design of all life,
shown in beauty as jewels and stars
and the lace of golden calligraphy.

And may you also see the pattern
of your own precious life
and how your life completes the design.

May all the choices you make
be grounded in wisdom.

May the light
of the One Beyond Names
touch your brow and your heart
and draw you ever closer
until you are home in love.

May the prayers of all who love you
lift you toward the light.
May their hands serve you.

And may your path be fulfilled,
now and in all the days to come.

Wandering

Wandering in the mountains,
following untamed rivers,
or within the walls of deep friendship,
opening secrets to each other—
there is nothing wilder than being alive.

All the experiences we live
boil up out of the pregnant void
and vanish.

We try to distill
this nectar of beauty and sadness
into a few words of power

and set them out as beacons,
as constellations, as gems, as offerings,
as medicine; while we, too,
follow in the footsteps of our ancestors.

Wind River Wilderness

A long paved road,
then a long dirt road,
then a long footpath
into the woods
and up into the mountains,
seeing almost no one—
has it been days now?—
then almost no path at all,
just a few searched-for cairns,
end at the outlet tip
of a slender, shining lake
rimmed by rippling marsh grasses
tinged with their autumn ambers and russets
and surrounded by a narrow band
of dark green fir and pine
held within a stark triptych
of gray granite walls
footed with slabs, boulders, and spall,
the centerpiece thrusting into the sky,
its abrupt thousand-foot face
a chunky and fissured eruption of gravity.

At this remote place
with its moist enclosure and tall tower
that echo the intimacy of creation,
we have traveled inward
as well as outward.

We find ourselves standing
on the shore of the great silence,
at the foot of the long wharf
that extends into the fruitful void,
at the place of arrival and departure.

Humbly, we notice
what we had missed
back in the marketplace:
the moment-by-moment
unspooling of eternity
right before our eyes.

Getting Down to Work
(Inspired by wisdom from the Haudenosaunee people)

As we gather here together,
may we be mindful that we all
have limited life spans and energies,
that every one of us desires happiness
for ourselves and for those we love,
that despite our powers
we are utterly dependent on the well-being
of the earth, our home,
on her soils, her waters, her green life-forms,
and all her other creatures.

May the wisdom of the four directions
steady our thoughts.
May the inner light
of high promise inspire us.
May the work we engage in today
be worthy of blessing from our ancestors
and be a source of eternal gratitude
from our descendants.

With full awareness of our imperfections,
we make our hearts and minds as one
to honor the web of trustful relationships
that holds us together as a people.

Now let us work to create
the simple beauty of what is needed.

Acknowledgments

The author gratefully acknowledges the following publications, in which some poems in this volume first appeared or are forthcoming: *Appalachia* ("Waterfall, Sounding"), *Front Range Review* ("Walking into the Foothills"), *Primary Point* ("The Eye of the Universe" and "It's a Funny Thing"), *Spiritus* ("Between Two Trees"), *Sufi Journal* ("There's a Place" and "Spiritual Landscape"), *Talking River Review* ("A Flight of Wings"), and *Witches and Pagans* ("Chakra Initiation").

An earlier version of "Advice from the Last Loon" appeared in the anthology *So Many Voices* (Poetic Matrix Press, 2017).

With love to my wife Susan Secord and our son, Benjamin, and deep bows to friends and colleagues who reviewed the manuscript: Bruce Allen, Cedar Barstow, Randy Compton, Leilani Rashida Henry, Francesca Howell, Peter Howell, Joe Hutchison, Steve Jones, Laurie Paulson, Richard Prée, and Ken Wachter.

About the Author

Chris Hoffman is an ecopsychologist and poet with a background in organization development (applied group psychology) and counseling.

Chris is the author of *The Hoop and the Tree: A Compass for Finding a Deeper Relationship with All Life* (ecopsychology/spirituality), now in its twentieth-anniversary revised edition, expanded with a key new chapter: "The Hoop and the Tree for Healing and Transformation."

Chris's poetry has appeared in his three previous books: *Cairns*; *Realization Point*; and *On the Way*, and also in national publications including *Appalachia*, the *Christian Science Monitor*, *The Climbing Art*, *Sea Kayaker*, *Spiritus*, *Sufi Journal*, and the *Chrysalis Reader*, as well as in the anthologies *The Soul Unearthed* and *EarthLight: Spiritual Wisdom for an Ecological Age* and *So Many Voices*. He enjoys performing his poetry both solo and in music and dance collaborations.

As an organization development consultant and licensed professional counselor, Chris has worked in a variety of clinical and organizational settings, including consulting with a Fortune 500 energy company (from union level to executive), counseling at mental health agencies, and teaching ecopsychology at Naropa University. He holds a BA from Yale University, a master's degree from Northeastern University, and an MBA from University of Colorado.

Now retired, Chris currently devotes most of his time to writing and to volunteer work for social justice and a livable climate.

Chris is a longtime practitioner of Zen and T'ai Chi and has studied traditional psychospiritual healing methods and sacred dance. His wilderness experience includes backpacking, mountaineering, sea kayaking, and river running. He and his wife live in Boulder, Colorado. They have one adult son.

Website: www.hoopandtree.org

Printed in the United States
by Baker & Taylor Publisher Services